A SPOKEN TRUTH

From Southeast Asia to United States of America

ADVOCACIES IN HAND
"No to Landfill"

An outcry that took me home

Written by:
NIDA GOUDEAUX

To order additional copies of this book, contact:
Xlibris
844-714-8691
www.Xlibris.com
Orders@Xlibris.com

ISBN: Softcover   978-1-6641-1928-4
        Hardcover   978-1-6641-1902-4
        EBook   978-1-6641-1901-7

Print information available on the last page

Rev. date: 09/04/2020

My power thoughts are sincerely dedicated to my ancestry and
my townmates in Alaminos, Laguna, Philippines.

I thank them all for accompanying us in our sacrifices and rallying behind and voicing a unifying
heroic strength of remarkable spirits to our advocacy of "No to Landfill." Together, we make history.

"MARAMING SALAMAT PO."

(Thank you in reverence.)

Introduction

For years, I was so detached from my hometown. I migrated to the United States in 1988 and was too busy exploring life and making a living. America became my home. But a provoking mission brought me back. Apart from the nostalgia of my childhood days, there's a spiritual clamor. Out of my own volition, through social media, I reached out to my townmates to get to know them, to awaken them and move them, to get their participation and involvement to my advocacy to fight and go against a project of Berjaya. It was hard enough to fathom that our small town, naturally abundant in trees and water bodies, one of Mother Earth's fine green environments, will be destroyed and covered by and dumped with truckloads of unimaginable toxic waste materials. The project targets to convert our small town into a landfill.

I have resolved to be involved, and I am determined to actively protest, "No to Landfill." I aim to help my townsfolk get through this journey to get better living conditions and not allow the dirty tricks, greed, and self-interest of those pro-landfill to bypass the will of the majority to preserve our town of beautiful sceneries and not have a large-scale sanitary landfill, proposed by Berjaya, a Malaysian company. I loudly express myself in social media, in a Facebook page called Alaminos, Laguna Association, which is exclusively participated by those whose origins, grass roots, and ancestry are traceable to our small town. It is a platform to express our sentiments, grief, disagreements, frustrations, and all emotions mostly against the landfill.

My brother joined the association ahead of me, and we were ones of the rallying starters to spread awareness, educate, voice out our advocacy, and make an impact to an increasing membership population. Some of our strongest supporters and valuable figures work behind the scenes, however strongly asserting our rights and our advocacy, "No to Landfill." This ongoing task has so far evolved immensely and aggressively with a very genuine intent of defending our town to flourish with integrity and further its growth as we formulate economic options to encourage investors to assist us accelerate our status to being a first-class municipality. Stagnation of growth has been obviously a big concern, but I believe the emerging situation of the proposed landfill by those in their confused state with souls lost in the dark enlightened the folks of Alaminos to finally rise and get involved in a most constructive manner.

I never imagined to write a book in this context, but it is a blessing in disguise, for there were no impediments and delusional reasons as to why not. It is historic to be engaged in a wide and passionate expression of democratic liberty to get through the power of words, insights and become the insightful power of encouragement to embellish and incorporate rallying works of achievements while those in power and bad influence to be cremated by the ashfalls of their dark beliefs and propositions mostly adhered by them.

Because of my compassionate and ever longing of coming through my departed grass roots of birth and to return to my heritage with prideful reincarnation to contribute something to a heritage mostly treasured—my involvement to some kind gestures in my own spiritual outcry opposing landfill at my loudest pronouncement –could be best collaborated by my own capacity and devotion to provide my strength and stretch it out to the finish line win a battle which is hugely and amazingly in devotional participation of the great majority residing in our home town as well as those who no longer are residing there locally and internationally to give their contribution either in tangible or intangible kinds or both---we will win through the heavy storms, the odds of times and the challenges confronting the town of so many issues and political agendas that are not in the eminent doctrine of the battling zone (protesting world of reality).

The people of Alaminos, Laguna, Philippines, set the tone toward this "No to Landfill," to look for the positive in all circumstances, and I am glad we are all united to fulfill progressing actions embraced by different advocating groups. I am so amazed by their creativity, brilliance, aggressive approach to rally a cause at their most dedicated and committed voice and action—there is that admirable confession of truth that prevails in this test of times.

"No to Landfill" will interestingly be a subject of spiritual enhancement in our own compassionate and comprehending mind-set. It could manifest within you an absolute truth, why we all got so involved and continue processing through the conclusive ending of such a quest for a lifetime victory. This is a remarkable story of a historic breakthrough that has never been this sensational, controversial, disturbing, and engaging but is absolutely, so amazingly advocated by an unexpected mass participation. The mass actions and upheavals of minds, where the strongest wavelength of liberal minds gathered on the street and rallied for a good cause, all widely pronounced and demonstrated, "No to Landfill," with the slogan printed on T-shirts and all over, chanting of the same cause and all sorts of expressing moods and gestures.

Our goal and advocacy "No to Landfill" is a great opportunity to be decisive, to be united, and to democratically exercise our freedom as responsible and faithful citizens as we honor and preserve our own heritage and culture upon a perfect haven of our paradise of treasures. Alaminos, GOD first!

Voices from all around the world, whose ancestry began from Alaminos, Laguna, spread like wildfire and thunderstorms, and everyone pretty much participated with compassion and rallying spirits at most. There are those more vigilant ones who are physically in our town and want to loudly air their sentiments and grievances, yet many of them are hindered by fears and anxieties, being that the powerful image of the politicos might stop them from being demonstrative.

However, on November 17, 2019, in a peaceful protest, "No to Landfill" courageously demonstrated on the street, determined to pronounce their objection. It was a success, and it inspired us to keep going. Strength and unity became our directive guideline of truth. There was joy and hope arising from an upheaval done in a calm display of emotions from the rallyists, but there was an episode where the sound system was not allowed to be used. A police officer put a stop to the use of the rented equipment, but a kindhearted fellow from the church volunteered to get the sound system from the church and be used in the rally instead. It was not a powerful audio system, but it did work out pretty well as the loud speakers for that moment.

There were anger, frustration, and commotion on the surface. However, it was tamed and pacified somehow with the logical position of the rallyists. They witnessed a retaliation to their use of their rented sound system, but it was resolved in an easy way, and the rally remained calm for the most part.

There was an amazing turnout of rallyists, and it was heartbreaking and emotionally touching. The quiet and simple town has no history of such an eventful upheaval, but finally, people spoke loud and stood firm on their advocacy: "No to Landfill."

It's amazing, admiring, and a great success, I must say. People's power culminates an even stronger reinforcement of heroism, and I salute everyone for their great participation. The Solid 6 has gone far and beyond what was expected. They echoed in their affixed truth of participation in black and white signatures, and I admire the tenacity and determination of an old friend in the Sangguniang Bayan who spearheaded the triumph from within his reach of influence and genuine service for what his moral responsibility and diligence calls for.

The participation from all parts of the world comes into one loud and clear pronouncement as our hearts and souls broke into pieces. Our treasure island will be transformed into a smoky mountain and will accumulate waste and toxic elements coming from all over our nation's largest dumpsites and be centered to and occupying our town premises. To begin with, it is not good to have a sanitary landfill of this scale. This is such a disgrace and dishonor to our heritage and very detrimental to standards of living. Such a toxic and destructive promotion for economic change by a prejudiced system is not ideal and not acceptable at all.

I strongly advocate against and object the proposal, which was strongly and seemingly embraced by the mayor himself and his faithful followers. To push for this landfill issue as an economic agenda is for their own self-interest. However, the Solid 6 in the municipal hall, as part of the decision-making body, crippled the "No to Objection." It was matched with a triumphant "No to Landfill," dominating the proposal and rejecting in absolute votes the most controversial and disturbing local issue of the landfill. Thanks be to GOD, our voices were heard, and the influence and the power of inner strength comes in a strong string of just and righteous stand from the admirable figures of genuine service. I applaud each and everyone who have made this fight against the landfill a true and heroic move toward a united front.

Alaminos, GOD first!

The Three Things

"Everything you even try to do to me; already done to you."

OPRAH WINFREY IS A MOTIVATIONAL SPEAKER I HAIL
UPON WITH UTMOST ADMIRATION AND RESPECT.

MY FREE WILL AND HIGH-SPIRITED LIVING CREATION

I CAME OUT WITH MY OWN PARTICIPATION OF TRUTH SPOKEN IN A LANGUAGE
PRODUCED BY MY MOST ENABLING EXPRESSION OR SELF-REVELATION.

This privileged speech from Oprah in the midst of a momentum in cue, just popped up.and here I was caught in a cheerful smile. All of a sudden and what are the odds when I was in the middle of intense emotions because the home of my ancestry and my own self---is in limbo and it is in complete disarray. I have been plugging in my posts via social media and this it caught me by big surprise and enlightened me to express myself even more with many revelations of my emotions revealed. Thus, collaborates even more from my inside and outside world. What are the odds and the challenges involved?

Imagine the impact and the intensity of my emotions, but I have overpowered myself to continue fighting and living with my advocacy. I did partner myself with convictions and wisdom at my heartful desires. Many throwbacks of good spirits join(ed) me in the effort of fighting against "No to Landfill." and I am in a positive mood though mixed with many surprises of disbeliefs and lies----hovered by many shadows of unrevealed nightmares, what a discovery? But together, with unity and good cause, we will emerge triumphant.

The strength of a voice speaks of advocacy---selfless and all. What I think is right and what is right is my ultimate response. No flaunting to criticize me from for I do speak my heart out loud enough in a circumstance that hits me from the bottom and up. This is such a mission dedicated for my self-proclamation but intended for my dire insistence to state my case. And I guess a reincarnation provoked upon me from my parents who had departed for many years now while in heaven they cheerfully did recognize the presence in a spirit engaged upon by me. This unique and true engagement is a precious, timely, and relevant gift with the events in my life. I never thought would be splurged in a story of my life projected in a scene of this historical event like this. But within my conscientious image, I have decided to participate my senses and spirituality with an open theory of my mind-set and all. My over-indulging and significant dramatic involvement in my lifetime is the revelation of what I always wanted to be. And, it is from a deep-well of what I feel is necessary and what I ought to be. Being there for those who need me most in my own little way to partner in any situation where I could become useful and be a reliever even in a brief or temporary relief. Truly indeed, I found my language of expression in my chosen speech. But in-depth and the true meaning it creates- no one should ever dare to calculate or undermine, just me. This is my own capacity of a treasure of mind gifted with my father in heaven shared upon me while I live it up with my own fill of honor and pride. My significant acceptance revealed by inspirations so immense. This is that heroic part of me---that engaged me in an advocacy, so called "No to Landfill." Back to my ancestral home---a heritage of my beginning to life that intensely invoked my participation to a maximum extent and through the loudest itch of my voice resonating with assertion of our democratic rights for the Love of our Paradise of Finest Green Environment and Natural Resources. Abound to be at our most preserved and abundant wealth so to speak.

There's no doubt that within me, there's an overflow of love and compassion. I am an ordinary woman but with enriching points of view and visions powered with actions in continuing such a missionary task. I ignore criticisms that do not add value in what I do, and I do not hold grudges. Rather, I expect understanding, love, and support in my choices. becomes unceasing. She has the sincerest voice of joy, flaunting without boastful intent, sharing the joy of being a winning participant in their life achievements. Such is a noble feeling with a prideful tone so invigorating and treasured—and this is exactly a personifying comrade in the fight against landfill where she provokes upon a mighty sword. It is armed with conviction and wisdom to challenge the tests of times----in a controversial and disturbing landfill issues confronting her ancestral town.

As a cancer survivor, the creation of a certain masterpiece of positivity and inspirational doctrines are manifested through prayers and experiences of many traumatic events. In the past, has driven her courageous spirit as her own form of relief anchored by redemption from the past and bitter struggles. Yet---best expressed in a vision so clear and a voice so loud with a heart so calm and soft. She aimed to accompany the rest of those who had suffered and those who are still fighting the co-called death-defying disease to not lose hope but rather become stronger and more courageous to face a destiny. With no doubts and no remorse but faith in their hearts that life will prosper in their own making guided by our Providence in His own special way. Be glad and be joyful. We are given the gift of life and a treasure of love. She hails upon herself with a Voice and a Sincere Heart belonging for "No to Landfill."

The emotional wholeness is best achieved by not allowing the weight of guilt and condemnation to be the wreckage of a refreshing start. The bitterness and negativity of your distressful encounters be a learning conservation of your productivity. In the next chapter of your adventure either you are in your own comfort zone or in your own exploratory zone. Make it an embracing thought. Be unceasing to discover what is the next goal or worth of space for the engine that will keep your motivation up and about. All that, depends on what you have truly experienced and that will give you many insights of "push overs" mechanisms. Such a derivative of life with many ingredients to spice the wheel of fortune as it moves in different directions, a choice that you will make. Just make sure prudence is your guiding light.

Personally, I do not engage much with excuses, for I find it useless and not sincere at all. I do try to live with grace, humility, and generosity as I search for more truth in me.. I have my own share of guilt, imperfections, and sinful thoughts but, I do try to not make excuses for myself. To say it is just but human, that we make mistakes is not acceptable. Having that kind of reasoning is not admirable. It is tolerating one's wrongdoings. We need to level up our thoughts. The best approach is to not entertain excuses that will invite more unrighteousness.

If we confess our sins, He is faithful and just to forgive us our sins

And to cleanse us from all unrighteousness

1 John 1:9 ESV

The lingering voice done in a slow pace could manifest skepticism, negativity and further contradictions. The real manifested scope of the person's heart and soul faculty reveals a heroic encouraging eco-growth and planning and greased upon it is a package full of a faithful paradigm with optimism and thrive to engage upon nature's bounties and humanitarian wealth in the long run. In short, an economic growth geared to accelerate mother nature's and our finest green environment to be utilized and promoted to the highest peak of a great sense of responsibility be tackled in a package yet still unknown. But, at the next chapter of it's true revelation will be tackled with objectivity and with a lot of sense. Let the creative and innovative wheels of fortune travel smooth in its own space and time and allow the perfect situation to restructure the necessity or urgency as it unfolds a new beginning and a new progress of a thriving solution. Let it be. Through the course of evolution to find it's way to get into perfect structure of time demand as it localizes towards more progressing liberty of many changes in our town at a more visionary creation of those contributing figures in the government authorities or agencies in placed.

Our powerful thoughts in biblical passages:

The Lord demands fairness in every business deal; he sets the standard.

Proverbs 16:11 NLT

The Lord despises double standards of every kind.

He is not pleased of every kind.

He is not pleased by dishonest scales.

Proverbs 20:10, 23 NLT

A spoken truth in many revelations from Southeast Asia to U.S.A. advocacies in hand (inspirational and motivational)---"No to Landfill" brought me back home—is a book written with a noble mission of a collaborating mind and soul within my own self philosophy of my ancestors behind me as I watch and listen to the voices of thousands of my town folks including myself in a applauding admiration of a beautiful gift of love of a precious paradise as I have always have honored my ancestry of my own belonging and the enormous blessings endowed upon me because every molecular evidence of genetic formation originates from my evolutionary standards enhanced upon my being. "No to Landfill"—brings me home as it brought me back home to my memory lane. So engaging and so affected by the clamor in hand that drives me to a high speed and intense awakening so that the good cause from an advocacy so well taken. It is increasingly highlighted upon a dominant voice could bring us all together to a cooperative spectrum of in a multitude of heavy weights and disposition of what we ought to accomplish at the end of the rainbow.

In social media for example, the FB (facebook) site centrally owned and with exclusive rights of limited exposure-thereupon is a voice so loud to shake this one mind in deep slumber and confront the challenges of a potential risk that could vanish the beauty of nature. And bodily sources in just one click of a stupid existence of landfill as to make Alaminos, Laguna, the dumpsites of toxicity in an unbelievable ghostly truckloads of waste products and live through mountains of grossed dumpsites all over the zones of our green and finest environment. What an embarrassing accommodation of a life living in a traumatic and death-defying production of stinky pieces of hazardous materials to get trapped from within the deepest ground through the top of the monstrous mountains of the highest peak of a calamity on a day-to-day basis. Such is a bizarre acceptance of economic disaster as opposed to economic growth so to speak—where the upheavals start to be protested via "Alaminos Laguna Association." A website that carries the latest news and the most useful tool of public consumption for everyone who wished/es to air their sentiments, grievances, opposition or support perhaps to landfill advocates but mostly---utilized for better views and reforms to accelerate to.

Because of the sensitivity of my emotion, I /had have actively participated in "No to Landfill" protest in an aggressive kind of action pronounced in social media and have spread my wings in bigger dimension too. I have thrown out my postings left and right for "Education and Awareness" and thus created some forms of stimulation being one of the courageous catalysts during the initial stage. And, even after to have increasingly skyrocketed a great number of membership due to great advocates that have subjected themselves (ourselves) to bringing out the best in our freedom of expression. As our democratic right and I must say with much prideful tone of being one very strong voice that has created an impact to magnetically invite more members to join---and thus convert my input even through some criticisms that were not valuable and worth a piece of argument to even tackle irrelevant matter. I have provoked and invoked better opportunities and learn many good examples of figures in our town for they have proven an immense point of views, discretion, will-power to participate more and contribute their skills of expertise with their most inspirational and motivational quotes and sayings. And even in narrative chapters did I ever imagine this will be the tile of my book----A spoken truth in many revelations from Southeast Asia to U.S.A. advocacies in hand (inspirational and motivational)---"No to Landfill" brought me back home-written in my most relaxing and even most hyperactive modes.

Enjoy my adventure as it brings you to my world of many passions, and in GOD's provision upon me of so many gifts of love and life, I could ever be so proud for I had my parents in their loving thoughts as I defend upon the possible wreckage of nature and human lives –along with me are all of you "No to Landfill" crying out loud---our support for this hard-long battle.

I aim to create a village where education and awareness are the core of interest and the village effectively becomes an organization of success. This is how our advocacy, "No to Landfill," started. From here on, we gathered a great number of people advocating for the same cause and who seem to be just waiting for a leadership to start a process of demonstration in a peaceful, faithful, yet mighty and courageous mass action to make many voices be heard.

In my point of view, the inevitable concerns occur when the spread of a silent commotion triggers the brilliant minds to internalize and diagnose the potential risks of landfill development as an introduction to business investment that will shake the tranquility and deep slumber of the little town so timid and remote in it's industrial and commercial structure--- and in some gentle gestures, there began a gradual awakening. There is a substantial evidence of a complete rejection or opposition against the venture of landfill (on a large scale by Berjaya)---in the person's fight for a democratic right and just of the people he truly serves. He has that subdued and gentle approach to disallow the accommodation of a possible landfill venture promoted by a gigantic corporate international to invade our hometown for it will pose danger in the lives of many and will destroy nature's beauty and green environment of a small town sitting in a quiet repose. Such is a puzzling and complicated approach to poke a sleeping beauty rest and in a grieving and despair route ---there is a time to get to keep moving in a direction to finally go through the motion of "disseminating information" in the most discreet way.

"The one strong voice of a gentle person resonates upon a genuine intent to organize a move towards unity in his subtle approach towards "No to Landfill," and not to be recognized for any entitlement, fame or glory---as to be propelled towards an aggressive move as he acts as a catalyst to aware the citizenry abandoned by some greedy creatures who thought they have the power to rise above all in their nightmares of sorrows dominating the choice of self-interest and betrayal to serve the public with noble tasks involved...

And I say,

"NO ONE CAN DESTROY A BEAUTIFUL SOUL."

(the truth will always prevail.)

Even if we are going through dark nights, our souls and tears entrapped by landfill issues, we are all in command of a spirit to come together in unity and set aside political and personal differences as we hold true to our advocacy to not limit ourselves to fight against the ill effects or epidemic of bringing toxic waste materials to invade a land of treasure. We have grown upon our finest green environment, and we won't allow destruction of lives and Mother Earth to prevail.

Voices from all around the world, whose ancestry began from Alaminos, Laguna, spread like wildfire and thunderstorms, and everyone pretty much participated with compassion and rallying spirits at most. There are those more vigilant ones who are physically in our town and want to loudly air their sentiments and grievances, yet many of them are hindered by fears and anxieties, being that the powerful image of the politicos might stop them from being demonstrative.

However, on November 17, 2019, in a peaceful protest, "No to Landfill" courageously demonstrated on the street, determined to pronounce their objection. It was a success, and it inspired us to keep going. Strength and unity became our directive guideline of truth. There was joy and hope arising from an upheaval done in a calm display of emotions from the rallyists, but there was an episode where the sound system was not allowed to be used. A police officer put a stop to the use of the rented equipment, but a kindhearted fellow from the church volunteered to get the sound system from the church and be used in the rally instead. It was not a powerful audio system, but it did work out pretty well as the loud speakers were utilized for that moment.

There were anger, frustration, and commotion on the surface. However, it was tamed and pacified somehow with logical position of the rallyists. They witnessed a retaliation to their use of their rented sound system, but it was resolved in an easy way, and the rally remained calm for the most part.

There was an amazing turnout of rallyists, and it was heartbreaking and emotionally touching. The quiet and simple town has no history of such an eventful upheaval, but finally, people spoke loud and stood firm on their advocacy: "No to Landfill."

It's amazing, admiring, and a great success, I must say. People's power culminates an even stronger reinforcement of heroism, and I salute everyone for their great participation. The Solid 6 has gone far and beyond what was expected. They echoed in their affixed truth of participation in black and white signatures, and I admire the tenacity and determination of an old friend in the Sangguniang Bayan who spearheaded the triumph from within his reach of influence and genuine service for what his moral responsibility and diligence calls for.

The participation from all parts of the world comes into one loud and clear pronouncements as our hearts and souls broke into pieces. Our treasure island will be transformed into a smoky mountain and will accumulate waste and toxic elements coming from all over our nation's largest dumpsites and be centered to and occupying our town premises. To begin with, it is not good to have a sanitary landfill of this scale. omi is such a disgrace and dishonor to our heritage and very detrimental to standards of living. Such toxic and destructive promotion for economic change by prejudiced system is not ideal and not acceptable at all.

I strongly advocate against and object the proposal, which was strongly embraced by the mayor himself and his faithful followers. To push this landfill issue as an economic agenda is for their own self-interest. However, the Solid 6 in the municipal hall, as part of the decision-making body, crippled the "No to Objection." It was matched with a triumphant "No to Landfill," dominating the proposal and rejecting in absolute votes the most controversial and disturbing local issue of the landfill. Thanks be to GOD, our voices were heard, and the influence and the power of inner strength comes in a strong string of just and righteous stand from the admirable figures of genuine service. I applaud each and everyone who have made this fight against the landfill a true and heroic move toward a united front.

ALAMINOS. GOD FIRST!

A man with a brilliant mind and clever actions in a genuine fulfillment (touched by an angel of an advocacy–– "No to Landfill."

A dominant figure --- in this particular fight and, this is my take on his phenomenal contribution. He acts as a master life with a clever mind put into actions. Not just with a brilliant brain. There is that engagement into weird situations that sharpen his knowledge to combat difficulties and more difficulties. As challenges begin with hitting some rock bottoms on the edges and re-group a systematic analogy of life-situation to come to a reasonable ground of creating is a solid foundation exasperated by some not attractive and blown out of proportions or some continual perils that drudged upon by later on eloquently climbed with tactics witty and reinforced due to more compromising institution of self-learning and vastness of discoveries. Channel upon understanding of his life-approaches as it is reinforced with realistic events experienced. No more scapegoats or sweet lemon defense mechanisms for it has consumed the most truthful revelation upon his own sight and coming through it in a visionary relevance and not by inhibitions executing a dominant contribution in his self-programming for now and the next time around eventful and drastic situations come to existence. There is that wisdom and call of his own conviction with family values at his most adhered factor of survival and decision-making at his most reasonable degree of conformity or compliance. The dictate of his genuine and conscientious heart prevails but being a tough "leader" is also a non-protesting proof of his righteous approach in any circumstance presented along his bridge of hope against sometime with some adverse or with severity of high degree of confrontations that could sometimes involve tricky and shocking approaches that are of surprisingly unique in nature. How could that be triggered by some obstacles not worth a finger to lift? Or should that be ignored just for the sake of being to burdens by unpredictable situations---not worth his time to be involved to? The man's calling as a duty or a mission to do the right thins---is of his pivotal interest and it is the right thing to do under an oath he promised. Or for the most part of his normal dictate of conscience---doing the right thing is the principle at will power of a choice he stood for or made.

I do salute this man, a friend I have reconnected from thousands of miles across both worlds on different point of horizons--our friendship has not vanished at all. It is by a heroic and non-defeating love of our heritage and culture and "No to Landfill" has strengthened our convoy of being under one spirit of advocacy. And, we both got so involved in our rallying conviction with a real vibes connection and with his great sense of influence and leadership under the umbrella of political issues being shelved under arrest but only with the real issue of landfill as the only focus.

God bless his heart and soul for a triumphant victory maneuvered and championed by his cleverness and brilliance at heart and soul. I thank him for a relief of sorrow thinking that our treasure island where we both belong will become a Landfill of a trashy and waste materials toxic and unhealthy to the residents occupying Mother Earth. It is a phenomenal victory hailed upon through his own dynasty of brilliant and clever structure upon his own dutiful right and best form of postured conviction and belief. And thus, proclaimed by his honest fist and reputation of his will power and moral responsibility. My heartfelt gratitude to a man I truly admire. "No to Landfill,"--- the sensational slogan or cry out in a remarkable history of a town, Alaminos, Laguna Philippines which has reached an end for a battle so inevitable and so unimaginable. We made it through heavy rains and thunderstorms hovered into darkness first thought "unknowns." And guess who authored the resolution recognizing the clamor, the rejection, of many of the townsfolk to not have a sanitary landfill on a large scale? It was this man with a brilliant mind and clever actions who appeased and pacified the fears and anxieties that had taken a toll on everyone's heavy heart and disturbed mind and soul.

Something Worth Sharing

My brother and I share the same sentiments and compassionate spirits on our same advocacy, with similar emotions of grief, despair, frustrations, as well as excitement and anxiety. We are both fearful of a possible sanitary landfill with unimaginable truckloads of trash to be brought into our town. This will pose extreme disaster to our town of "Alaminos" and will destroy the beauty of this town sitting in the paradise of nature's best.

My brother and I heeded the call to step up for this mission to educate and make our fellow "Alaminos" folks aware of the dangers of the landfill. Our goal was to get the attention of our people and focus on our position, "No to Landfill." We presented many facts and emotional sentiments in an open platform in social media, in a group called "Alaminos Laguna Association." We succeeded in inviting members to join the fight. We are one of the few who heralded and spearheaded this advocacy to oppose the landfill project of Berjaya.

We are glad the program of action made and participated by us and those of you in Alaminos and all over and across many horizons and those who had left our town and are still in the Philippines with similar background of ancestral kinship under one strong mission. We will still be strong advocates and we are always in the same dilemma just like everyone who feels this is such bad news for us. At some point be able to gladly see better resolutions and be assured that those in power and influence in the Municipal Hall finally come to the conclusive and compromising stand of winning our battle "No to Landfill" but only to take care of our own trash.

There is no collaboration of mind sharing ---we both engaged into but we are in the same light of fighting for what is right and just and we thank you all for allowing us to be partners in the greatest love for "Alaminos, Laguna." No to Landfill" ——our everlasting movement to a glorifying and historical event of our genuine advocacy.

The Beginner In His Own Command

Right from the start of "No to Landfill"
Comes a voice resounding, brave and full of strength
There is goes his technical expertise in disseminating facts
With logic, validity, and professional background that completes
The whole package of his steadfast belief through the entire arena
Of "No to Landfill" being his truest advocacy
The gentleman involved has no self-interest for fame and glory
He had magnified his enormous capabilities enriched through time
There is no doubt about his efficiency, for he had advanced his own
System of his dynamic world in the field of engineering and the
Application in the business world he had so far explored
There was a tremendous amount of successes embarked in his
Own business career, and he never stopped engaging further
As his destination offers many greater opportunities as he lives through
Another world of paradise, USA becomes an immigration of truth
Where every detail of livelihood pertains to economic changes and
The new journey becomes a fruitful engagement more to contemplate
With higher perspectives in hand to stunning and amazing growth
Of prevailing many challenges and circumstances but classified by him
As a "no brainer" because his excellence in being a trusted fighter
In any game plans of serious endeavors
Are indulged by him in many analytical and prudent scrutiny
The gentleman at his advocacy statements begun with basic steps

"No to Landfill"---Outlined upon identifying the problems
And collected data to document the problem pertinent and all
Gathered support and suggested leadership be in command
Across the country where the municipality is involved
Alaminos, Laguna, Philippines, the defining subject of issues concerned
Mapped out a timeline of activities relevant to the cause
As he empowered resounding communications and activities
In the so-called education and awareness—to be the start up
Of our rallying protest to succeed "No to Landfill"—being his most
Engaging modus operandi in the social media of "Alaminos Laguna Association"
Being the most useful forum of exchange of communication
In our exclusively website of choice, a public consumption
Designed to disseminate information and whatever relevant theories
Necessary to include in the successful campaign of "No to Landfill"
There goes in a courageous voice of assertion and democratic liberty
A voice of a man---Powerful and Logical in his affiliation to an advocacy
"No to Landfill"—his leadership campaign begins to prosper with
Amazing increase of membership of which he has been the greatest catalyst
To make a difference in his discerning choice of wisdom and conviction
A true nature Alaminos heroic figure in his own right and approach---
A fighter, a real genuine, a brilliant and a sincere captivating man of strong voice
With a vision of economic progress to finally target our domain of stagnation
And upgrade our municipality and no longer be in a third-class category
It could be properly handled with better structure of mindset
To begin and be refreshingly managed by the powerful authorities
Mandated in their (public servants) moral duty of serving our town.

The set of leadership to achieve to empower others to achieve a collective efforts and goals rely on having one. His voice lead a strong participation and motivated a great many to give their contribution; tangible and intangible both assets produced.

Inspirational leadership comes not by an impulse
It is preserved with motivational goals from within committed cause
And a clause of conviction and of wisdom
Being of strong evidence of truth uphold

Your aspirations are opportunities
And are endeavored by life-changing creativity greater than challenges at hand

---

Do not allow bad habits to invade your head
Let it be occupied by many spaces where higher thoughts become the potential key
To a pocket of happiness now and the futures

The number one quality to make
Is not to allow abundance blocks to be at your doorstep
Rather allow the strength of many blessings
To dominate the work of creations

Steadfast, resilience, tenacity, vigor, and wit
All comes in living colors
Encompassing the many challenges and odds
Exceeding mostly by an act of genuine tasks
And guiding upon by faithful love
Defined heroic in an arm cradled by grace
And by a cheerful imposed of a refreshing start of new dawns
"No to landfill"---stays forever in a sanctuary where there is nothing
Left but a healing emotional unrest that has pacified
Or yet to be persuaded by more affirmations still left more to regain the trust
Of an avenue momentarily shaken by many rigorous steps
In an intellectual setting where the combat of attack is proven in the heart
of those with abundant gift of life----where the pocket of treasures
is an embarked instrument of a fighting victory

Learning to live a refreshing life begins with living with
a healthy mind, a beautiful soul, and a peaceful heart.

My goal is not to be better than anyone else
But to be the best I could ever be in my own sanctuary of self-progression

---

When thinking about life, the act of believing in yourself is a responsibility to consider
But take all the risks because winds travel in different directions
Such is a kind of journey as many seasons of life do take
Just make sure every passing time is engaged in meaningful ways

---

Be yourself and be the best you can be
Offer your whole being with pride and honor
To signify a life of worth that makes a difference
And come up with a legacy to build you up through a lifetime
That could define "YOU" best.

The quality essential to success
Is knowing first your weaknesses
And transform the learning driving machine to accelerate you
Towards making a strength to enforce your will power
And make a commitment of a promise due upon YOU

Special People and Special Dreamers

Love is part of everything
This is the gift of life
Special people are special dreamers as well
They have the sincerest and most compassionate heart
Where the space is unlimited, so wide and so inviting
They work together in many gracious ways
Positive thoughts in life presents all that is pleasant
Where special people and special dreamers are in one
Set of mindset and heart in control
And hold no remorse of the bitter past
And approach the future with no mysteries involved
They flourish upon the fundamental truths and
Ignore the complexities with objective responses
For they are special people and special dreamers
With emotional wholeness as their spiritual command
Of time-changing evolutions

Time Is On Your Side

A perfect situation to redeem yourself from miseries inflicted against your people
Time moves forward whether you resist or not
We can change our opportunities as we savor challenges
But let the inhibitory changes be the advocate of your own free will
To taste the appetizing new direction
And not know the "unwanted" and the "not-reconciling" adventures
Of the not pleasant and losing battle of your selfishness
Be the moral image of consciousness in a living trust of your legacy
You ought to embrace and uphold.

Lord, you are all over my life
You created me for a purpose
I never thought I would be
For benevolence of heart
Is a virtue that brings out the best in me
In your chosen beautiful destiny for me
To shine upon my heart and soul
A gift forever so kind to share

The perfection of human nature
Is seen in the embodiment of a kind loving soul
And to continue and fulfill a vocation of a selfless heart
Such is a gentle approach of sharing joy and
In a bosom plate of faith and love
For it is upon the act of believing on it and kindness
That savors the tranquility and content of life as it swings
Upon the many highs and lows as it proceeds
And resonates upon a good sense of a complete emotional wholeness
In such a fashion of a perfect spiritual approach of human kindness
And in many loving gestures as truly expressed, such is the beginning and an end
In the many acts of benevolence embraced upon a prayerful idealism
The exercise of benevolence is undoubtedly an act of self-willing
That expects nothing in return
But it is an exchange of a trade of joy and compassion
Over an act of giving an overflow of an enriching soul
Where GOD proclaims the pleasing conduct of a manner rejoining
Upon a gracious gift where love and commitment so precious and noble awaits
The triumph of an advocacy mostly fought for
No to landfill"--an outcry invoked
In a loud impact whereby
Education and awareness created the awakening call in

My most proactive gesture of a mission
Best uphold

To feel much for others---is a task as a commander in chief
Of one's own promulgated principle by an act of benevolence
Where a belonging heart
Does recognize the reasonable capacity to give in
And unmindful yet of any invaluable criticisms
For there is that calling of sharing in a mission of once in a lifetime
There comes a fulfilling avenue of an advocate free willing self
In a historicalevent prevailed in progressing actions of a legacy ---of one's stronghold and all.

Bible study is a spiritual enrichment
It covers a great magnitude about living and loving
Of sharing and having GOD as the center of all our daily tasks
And many more to know, to learn, and to discover
As we all bring ourselves in the likeness of GOD

In GOD, I trust
Your loving kindness extends to heaven
Your teachings, my guiding light

God pours His blessings on us
Especially those who have humble heart
God continues to provide more graces
As we stay committed to our dear LORD in the service of mankind

And surrender our spirit in the fullness of our LORD, Jesus Christ.

As we glorify our LORD Jesus
We have achieved that satisfaction within our souls
As we glorify GOD in eternal covenant
As we surrender our body in the holy kingdom, a paradise heaven that is.

Every day is a new and brighter endeavor
An opportunity to know more of GOD
As we glorify GOD in a purpose of a righteousness
To live in peace and harmony
And share the beauty of life
As we live in the grace of GOD

I want to be an epitome of "inspiration"
So that when they look at themselves, they can claim I have been an inspiration
For the thriving actions that allow many opportunities
To be their driving force to sharing life
Graciously and kindly without any signs of rejection
There are glad tidings in the sharing of love and life

My most driven purpose is to become rich
Rich in fun, rich in love, rich in laughter, rich in knowledge
Rich in sharing, rich in all kinds---that is good
And rich in learning from the bitter past and all
To be rich in love and life-sharing is achieved
For I am rich in the eyes of GOD

Life is much less complicated
As we discover the truth in us and from within
As we learn to know the purpose of living and the true meaning of life
And this is when we begin to make a difference in our own standard of living
And a legacy worth our significance

The earth is full of riches
I explore the potentials presented upon me
And to deliver without a single doubt
Abundant blessings be at my most harvest time

I have fought a good fight; I have shared the fruits
Of my persevered and noble heart

I will continue my mission
I will expand my horizons
To different outreach programs to help those in need
And upon this humble spirit of gratitude
To enjoy a life of plenty
And let SHARING be the most fulfilling act of moral responsibility
I hold a commitment, a promise of no denial
To be as genuine and as faithful
For a missionary task in the name of the LORD, our GOD. AMEN.

Let Your Soul Yearn for Truth in Your Own Discovery

Living an inspiring life
Begins at home
And it explores through the outside world
At the end of the day, our soul speaks of truth
There is no denying there is that amazing heights
Of reflection---smart and dazzling as the stars
There is that thanksgiving of discovering the yearning
At some point, soul search becomes the easy way
To reconcile and compromise——there is that revelation
Inside the life's truth meaningful beliefs
Out of honesty and sincerity it brings on as "YOU"——
Let your soul yearn for truth in your own discovery
Just be smart and be prudent for your conscience
Will speak better for YOU.

We Have the Power to Choose What We Feel Is Right

True, the wind travels in different directions
We have no control over that element the zones have to go
This is like choices in life---
We have different ways crossing paths and cross overs
We have different choices we make or to choose from
Happiness and content is our choice to make
We have that power of control to decide which way to go
Let that wind in our face or in our being dictate to us
Where it blows per our own remarkable option
Of an adventure in life that we should own
For ultimately, we have the power to choose what we feel is right
And let us follow what we feel is right and just.

Nida Bejosano Goudeaux

As I ponder upon and reflection comes to mind, I close my book of many chapters inside life---I open new pages as new beginnings to prove a new fresh start and a new soul upliftment as New Year is about to re-invent a new "ME" with better and new opportunities since New Year's Eve is about to commence a new dawn.

From a threshold of faith and cheerful thoughts---there upon lies a bundle of joy and faith expected to shine through for it is the tranquil liberty of a choice to dream about as it brings peace and content with changes processing as it internalizes the very core of my innermost---my soul and my BEING to begin with.

New Year 2020 is a new slate to refresh a new Life....it holds no bars of regretful engagement, it invokes a change of mind in a dictate of conscience-- a pleasing reflection to GOD's desire in our story of life conceived by an everlasting love without any fragmented notations.

Let us try to build a dream and a pyramid of a chapter with a book of legacy to reveal there is an image of GOD's creation destined to prove the truth of life with greater sense of maturity and responsibility in an enabling tasks of many kind gestures, gratitude and love for one another and uplift manifolds of true spirits in new resolutions empowering a celebration of love and life.

As I gather the facts behind---no regrets, no remorse, no bitterness but many lessons learned as a fresh start of a new world for a NEW YEAR'S eve, a welcoming of my religious and moral duty to be GOD's daughter in many cheerful rhymes....and in a swing of flickering and blasting dancing lights to become a living fact of a head start to a prelude welcoming and best attended by my own new world. Perhaps not much of adjustments to make as I am accustomed to this authenticity of life's program as I staged it as my very own paradigm combined with many learning curves. This is my own vocation of a non-isolated situation with better perspectives too engaging after all--in my own opinion and, I, be glad in God's another gracious way.

Thank you for a year blessed and a new day to start upon the greatest New Year's Eve breakthrough with a musical hymn of a love so faithful and all. GOD bless everyone and Happy New Year....2020, our luckiest year charm!!

May our heritage culminates the very best-- in many progressing advocacies and realities. GOD bless Alaminos, Laguna, Philippines, Italy and America---and the whole new world!!!

Again, HAPPY NEW YEAR and may the good Lord showers all the wonderful blessings---Love and Peace to mankind.

Salamat po. (Thank you in reverence.)

Superstardom complex is a no-show adhering fact to prevail
It is against the noble embedded self-display of one's being
In a struggling fight of a democratic right
Begin to encourage upon more increasing participation and not to carry any weight
To break down unity but build up more hopes
And allow the freedom of success and the liberty of admiring responsible
And moralconscience of what today brings and the tomorrows of the next ones
Of many generations to follow in one's super advocacy
NO TO LANDFILL" BE THE GREATEST LOVE OF ALL In
many respectable manners as LIFE begins to go on
In many respective invocations of worth-while living in GOD's presence and all
Alaminos,Laguna----a town so truly loved by us

There is no guilt and condemnation that will shout upon and loud
Maybe that entrapment of darkness that hovered lost souls
Was once a test of times
Redeem yourself with a confession of sincerity
Where in your silence you there is that privileged sound of a giving in
To an advocacy---a good cause beneficialto all
Including yourself once in a realm of disarray,confusion and self-vesting interests
Not a rule of life to follow or to obey after all.

I am truly fascinated by other people's creativity, good heart, and productivity. The brilliant mind enhanced and partnered by their actions in progress is really a big strength and admiration that I dearly challenge myself with more yearnings and desire to be at a fruitful labor of developing myself even further than what I would like to imagine... There is not a single inch of envy or jealousy in me, but it is an awe of their achievements that dominates my sensitivity and my developmental theory built upon my dream world of materializing and making a difference while I climb mountains where I will be able to stand above the highest peak and can proclaim with pride and honor. I have reached the direction of fulfillment from the dreams of my own reality of existence without any hesitation as I work in progress through a changing infusion of prevailing circumstances that has driven me more to come and true as in a standing ovation of my own making. Thus, is a commitment I pronounced with a modest interest engulfed upon me.

I truly admire the mastering spirit and ingenuity of a man I know has eloquently spelled the progressing lifestyle of his chosen world. Politics is a work of art in a spectrum so complex, controversial, but trademarked by better ideologies and program of actions to a fulfilling and beyond doubt of here and now. Such is a stigma that I could not adjust or engage into but the dynamic constituency is the prevailing magic of a person I know is living a legacy and a content of giving his entire dedication to a possessing nature of his goal-setting. Such is open mind and on-going mastering ability of his own service and duty of choice. All that I can utter---I am proud of you. But the endurance and tolerability persona and level of involvement is unlimited and unconditional which is in a true sense a passion and a mission and a calling that everyone has to engage or is gifted with such a prowess of their most attributed advocacy of missionary privileges. I prefer to reference as their point of their truest color. But not all of them in their constituency are adopting or have that inherent factor of truth in them. The gentleman I refer to is gifted and determined to comply with the rules of law and the rules of life progression.

There goes the project of senior citizen community services of which I could take part in donations and other forms of easing the lives of the elderly. The strength and the extension of my livelihood becomes an easy yet enduring task because the caregiving or the board and care is my biggest advocacy of my economic security. And this is where I give my full time and dedication to provide excellent care and hands-on involvement in the real sense of the business nature of this type of operation. I can just leave the tasks to my staff and people I trust but I have decided to make sure my involvement is at a maximum degree for me to be able to satisfy the very sensitive and the very delicate part of their lives. To provide quality care and utmost services and being compassionate is a heartfelt gift of dignity to someone reaching the end of life. Indeed, is my living treasure of my dedicated legacy so engraved in my greatest form of joy and content that involves a stronghold of faith, love, compassion and patience as my invoking arm of anchorage. I live by faith and by the love of GOD dwelt upon me and I will forever be grateful for whoever has defended the helpless and who unselfishly devoted an honorable services and act of compassion and is very humane in performing his duty to life manifesting in a heroic gestures of his own deliberate and honest contribution. I am committed to be in a silent partnership of simple giving and dignifying the aged in their comfort zone at the end of life and providing my support for giving dignity and quality care at my most enabling capacity.

There is a visionary symmetry n our work of minds and liberty of choices to prosper the missionary task endowed upon a wishful inner strength as we focused on more developing and calculating circle of expansion. To better the recreation and occupational programs of actions is within his interest of advocacy. To exhibit the dream come true march of attendance and coordinate with the demands of their needs (the elderly)---we need to put extra efforts and invest more resourceful ways to broaden the magnitude of activities and changing reflexes to enhance and prolong their life-span through an active adventure engaged in in-door and outdoor exercise. Such is a statement not to be undermined with a degree of doubt or non-assertion to the principle of enjoying it. While it is a motivation of a power mind in coordination with muscles involved and cognitive faculty enhanced and still progressing in each own scope of functioning---his mighty advocacy is propelling.

Lastly, I hope the senior citizen center will provide safe parks and a wide variety of recreational activities and opportunities. It surely will be a home where they can discuss and participate in socialization and encourage the elderly to still actively be engaged in many areas of destination, fun and games within the borders of the premise built for them.

Nida Bejosano Goudeaux

2 hrs

The Very Beginning Stage of "No to Landfill"

A gentleman and a dear friend (brilliant and full of strong convictions and from our town also) I had a chat with today asked me, "What can you say about Alaminos?" I was stunned, but here it goes:

"Alaminos as it's finest Green Environment will never be a lost paradise in a flinch of a stroke of a pen to vanish and lost of the beauty of nature and the pristine flow of water in rivers and bodies of water abundantly endowed upon by the grace of Life." To this, we shout out LOUD in a majestic freedom of our one voice, one spirit, one community, "No to Landfill."

Nida Bejosano Goudeaux

Modérateur • 16 h

Magandang hapon po sa inyong lahat.

I did hear the speech of the administration this morning (via a video clip forwarded to me by some friends/advocates of mine), and he said, "Dream big and I am a dreamer." Beautifully constructed line of your speech I listened to, and I would personally applaud you for that because you also mentioned you want something beautiful for Alaminos, and I will add another plus sign in your privileged inspirational sharing. This is for you, and I utter, "Maraming salamat po."

More than two weeks ago, I mailed a letter via US Priority to to the administration, and I did post in here in our site. I hope it had enlightened him somehow, but allow me this opportunity again to add more, and here it goes:

1. Life is beautiful and could be more beautiful. A dream does not become reality through magic. It takes patience, hard work, and sweet courage to fulfill.

2. Goal-setting is ageless and limitless. What is started today is never finished tomorrow but aim to lead you to a path where there is trail of a moonlight upon a dawn of a beautiful life and results.

3. A dreamer never fails to envision productivity and keeps on the strength of changing his/her world or the world he/she lives in with the passion of bright stars to keep on going and thriving for excellence.

In my own structuring motivational dreamer staircase to a heaven of joy and the beautiful art of shaping "Alaminos" I will join you in your dream where there is no space of imagination ever from hereon. "No importation of basura"

You did mention that it is mandated by DENR that every municipality and city to have sanitary landfill. Good news, that means, every city and municipality has that big responsibility of taking care of their own "basura" and that is very defining and even more concrete. "Alaminos" should never ever allow importation of "basura." no more excuse(s) why we be responsible for other region's toxicities and waste eliminations. Not in "Alaminos" not in our book to follow, for "Alaminos" should preserve it's perfect beauty and the easence of a green haven of many hopes and aspirations. Live and enjoy and seek better options.

Dream big, and it is Free, but your dream is so precious to us as well as to yourself, and being the leader of our town, keep that strength of your dream as a dreamer and as a model of productivity and in keeping Alaminos beautiful. Keep your music alive as you continue to dream big and join us in our most historical dream ever. "No Importation of Basura." And let it be the rhythm of a storyline in an embarking episode of your most concluding dream of a legacy to share upon your people, and we will all be glad we made it through struggling activities.

Maraming salamat po. GOD bless.

Nida Bejosano Goudeaux

Modérateur • 32 min

"A bitter refrain is not a remedy to a fight for a great rallying advocacy. Focus on positivity . . . a unifying spirit and a word of wisdom uplifts the integrity of a visionary mission . . ."

Wake up with a cheerful pose and approach a daily living with a morning delight that savors the sweet taste of life . . . GOD bless.

Susan Fandiño Vivid, lucid, and positive . . . Well said!

Egay De Villa þ Nice. The message is very healing. Let's move on very productively.

Nida Bejosano Goudeaux þ kaya nga . . . parang capitalization or impact is focused on the history and story line of bashings---it seems vengeance is just boiling from within . . . can it not be a sorrow of the past and be buried? Move on and carry the torch of advocacy without any qualms of bitterness, speculations but instead an honest approach to fight a good and just cause to life-living in Alaminos? But, make sure there is that logic and wisdom of truth---and no ulterior motives whatsoever...election and campaign has it's own timeline . . . "No to Landfill" is the greatest honor of our image and a defining legacy one holds with the clean and pure intent of a dream fulfilling and all . . . Di ba Egay we are always on the same page ha??? Tama tayo dyan . . .

Nida Bejosano Goudeaux

Modérateur • 6 h

Our greatest advocacy is anchored by a steadfast and a powerful voice of a love for "ALAMINOS" and will remain as such. GOD bless.

Nida Bejosano Goudeaux

Modérateur • 7 février, 16:19

I am deeply honored to be a part of our advocacy, inspired by an ideal and a tranquil approach toward better reforms or changes. We all embrace the privilege of being under one citizenry, one spirit of love for one another in our dream toward progress and to offer to the next generation the pride and honor of being from "Alaminos," either through birth or newly acquired residency or whatever possible way of affiliation there might be.

Just remember, the good reputation and the image of our most unifying spirit is an inspiring part of our history. The next generation will look upon us with pride and honor for being a true-blooded Alaminosian, authenticated by an ancestry supported by an assertive and a firm conviction to rebuild our town with a shining legacy of a united freedom of assembly rallying upon a pursuit of prosperity and economic changes. Such is a gift of life of a living legacy which truly belongs to us in our most humble and dynamic set of hope driven by concerted efforts which is characterized by our greatest aspiration. This is just the beginning of a one life to live, whereby all the heroic efforts demonstrated truly counts and let there be light at the end of the tunnel.

Alaminos, GOD first!

Nida Bejosano Goudeaux

Modérateur • Hier, à 12:36

A universal concept or applicable matter-of-facts.

Agricultural land-use conversion, either for commercial or industrial purposes.

1. Reclassification of land use/usage should be specified, and it should be explained in detail the utilization for land use conversion with plan and development included and governing agency/ies to undertake such (i.e., local government unit, etc.)

2. Titling process—to verify there is no cloud on title. Clear and perfect to protect the owner and the buyer (investors, etc.). A mutually beneficial ownership and transfer of title and make sure there are no flaws or clear of title is achieved.

3. Building permit which specifies the occupancy or intent—local standards need to be complied to; land use, zoning, and construction; to allow construction and ensure protection, safety, and entitlement application, either residential or commercial, industrial, etc.

(The rules and zoning regulations are submitted in the project application and design and should meet the zoning standards and pass the environmental review as well.)

Zoning permit is a mandatory requirement for any land use, whether it is a new, expanded, or revised/changed status, and it should be made available prior to issuance of a building permit. In other words, for land use under this specific intention of agricultural conversion, this is a standard practice or compliance to meet the applicable laws.

There should be security of performance, especially during the construction period, and should be included in the application part of the process.

Guys, if you see a backhoe, do not be alarmed. Make sure we are guided with this applicable law, which I strongly believe is a compliance for the most part, any part of the globe, and Philippines is not an exception.

I just want to impart my know-how, especially on this specific subject, as a realtor myself. As mentioned, this is a universal theory or practice and facts in the world of real estate and, in specific, land use. I hate to say this—reactions tend to be alarming whenever one sees a backhoe on a job site (to-be), and without sufficient information or evidence to know and understand the land-use intent, this becomes a concern for all, especially because of landfill issues that had been/are disturbing the township. There are things to consider and understand at its most objective and logical setting of minds after all.

I hope there are some clarity that can appease our emotions in times like this.

Thank you and GOD bless.

Nida Bejosano Goudeaux

Modérateur • 6 h

As long as we stay focused and dedicated to our advocacy---something worthy to cherish in life is to embrace the significance of a good cause which is prosperity and not to destroy the integrity of Alaminos and to triumph upon many dreams, and there is no way we could go wrong if we live upon our expectations.

Nonetheless, be reminded, petty situations are not the relevant matter-of-facts to give priorities to. To establish and enhance better connections and better rapport with others outside our own circle of a mission we are involved with, hopefully though can promote and can bridge the gap to a vision where good storylines and exchange of views with a privilege to express the true nature of one's belief or convictions and bring upon a living legacy to engage into one mutually beneficial interest to be shared upon...The rest are remarkable sense of respect and cooperation and sharing of intellectual topics adhered to establish a victory with high hopes for "Alaminos" and thereupon, create an image of love for each other and a spirit of belonging which should be our starting and endless standpoint for a united stand of freedom. There should be no intent to depart from the true nature of our rallying advocacy, and any form of engaging communications should continue within the realm of productive interaction and better navigation, vis-a-vis a direction toward better perspectives and greater vision should be our guideline.

And I think those in the chamber of the local government should also have the same line of advocacy— for the betterment of all. I am optimistic we can settle our differences with compromising acts of better resolutions and compromise to better understanding.

Let us all join hands together and gear our efforts for a common goal—for Alaminos to become a prosperous municipality—and set aside personal or political differences. Always remember, "Unity is strength, division is weakness."

God bless Alaminos and everyone.

Nida Bejosano Goudeaux

Modérateur • 14 février, 15:53

Good morning/afternoon, everyone. Please spend a minute or two. Thank you.

The signature petition letter "laban sa basura" authored and dedicated by BIGKIS was delivered to different and respective government agencies (DENR, DILG, Office of the Mayor, etc.) and in fact, it was the most ideal approach done in a legal and ideal way as far as we are concerned. It was not acknowledged or received by the mayor himself, but that was all right because it will be ignored or trashed anyway. The Office of the Vice Mayor received it, and that was okay too. No big deal, and it did not cause any negative impact on our part as advocates—not a bit!

The most significant task has been concluded somehow, and this means they could not railroad the certificate of "No to Objection" in the barangay council and SB (Sanguniang Bayan), and this is a protective step that perhaps the Office of the Mayor neglected or ignored to consider. Having said that, the demeanor demonstrated by him only proves one thing—our most desired objection or resistance to landfill development is totally a nuisance to him and our advocacy seems negligible as far as he is concerned. That attitude simply tells us the mayor, though he was suggesting for a dialogue, will only accommodate "No to Landfill" participants/attendees just so there was a formal invitation to have an open forum. This social-engagement-to-be (dialogue) is moot and futile as far as I see it. Such a hypocritical and insincere gesture coming from that highest hierarchy of power! The platform where we are all engaged is clear and concise—"No Basura"—just our own municipal "basura," period. There is that concept, such as an open-door policy, perhaps in his mindset, that will never go away. There is money and progress in "basura" to uplift our municipal status (?) and for other personal vested interest (?), but this is not what the citizenry of Alaminos was demanding immensely and ideally from him. Oh well, what are his options? It is up to him, but the future will decide, and the kind of legacy he was crying out loud will dictate at the end of his tenure or whatever and will figure out the kind of performance which will further elaborate the true nature of his being and especially him as a public servant.

The truth will define his own ground rule as far as this challenge goes and how he defends his people against all odds, if there is love and compassion still left for the people he is ought to serve, which, to me, is kind of leary and doubtful to many.

So far, there is no pilottage, no investors, no applicants, and we can, for now, be calm and at peace to accept there is no negative shadow within our reach—for now. But stay vigilant (not be a pest either), and we will finally succeed this game plan hopefully that has once trembled and rattled our township for a while now. Transparency is still our number one relevant, matter-of-fact demand. Let us hope and pray the governing body will finally settle to a concrete manifestation of their spiritual convictions as well. There are some of them that are within our reach of advocacy, but others are deemed too unclear and uncertain or trapped by some cloudy spirits. We remain hopeful for a better change of hearts (by some of the members of the governing body), especially this Valentine's day.

GOD bless you all.

Mountains could mean so many things
They could be scary and encapsulate your greatest adventure
Meaningful stories to tell and treacherous acts possibly to exist
But on a positive note, there is that triumph above that mountain high
Where the journey of life fascinates through the grandiose height and there is that
Thrill of the summit that captures the advocacy at hand
Through the struggles and pains of time
And connotes upon a climbing adventuring production
The magnificent and heroic echo as the mountain sings together for joy with the LORD
Upon your shoulder to believe, to hold and to grow
MT. PATAGIN––I never thought I would take even a glimpse
And into this mountain and indeed in my imagination did I find my soul
There is that calling that I should go to come and see it
A mountain is sincere and as you climb the highest peak
Dreamlike memories are articulated within reach on a mountaintop

Nida Bejosano Goudeaux

Modérateur • 3 janvier, 21:15

Be encouraged to bring one's capacity to fight for our own advocacy.

Light the candle of "No to Landfill" strong ability 4 Alaminos be encouraged to bring one's capacity to fight for our own advocacy

Nida Bejosano Goudeaux

Modérateur • 3 janvier, 10:51

Magandang umaga pong muli sa inyong lahat.

Lahat po tayo "No to Landfill" ay nagumpisa sa ating magandang hangarin para sa ating bayan—, kalikasan, kabuhayan at kalusugan ay ating mapangalagaan–samahan po natin ng walang sawang pagmamahal at pagkakaisa. Lahat po tayo ay nanindigan sa magandang adhikain para sa bayan----at dapat po nating panatilihing ang ating adbokasiya ay maging isang malinis at panatag na tungkulin tungo sa ating minimithing tunay na tagumpay at samahan ...

Nida Bejosano Goudeaux

Modérateur • 16 h

Magandang hapon po sa inyong lahat.

I did hear the speech of the administration this morning (via a video clip forwarded to me by some friends/advocates of mine) and he said: "Dream big and I am a dreamer.." Beautifully constructed line of your speech I listened to and I would personally applaud you for that because you also mentioned you want something beautiful for Alaminos and I will add another plus sign in your privileged inspirational sharing. This is for you and I utter--"Maraming Salamat po."

More than 2 weeks ago, I mailed a letter via US Priority to the administration and I did post in here in our site...I hope it had enlightened him somehow....but allow me this opportunity again to add more and here it goes---

1). Life is beautiful and could be more beautiful...A dream does not become reality through magic---it takes patience, hardwork, and sweet courage to fulfill.

2). Goal-setting is ageless and limitless--What is started today is never finished tomorrow--but aim to lead you to a path where there is trail of a moonlight upon a dawn of a beautiful life and results.

3). A dreamer never fails to envision productivity and keeps on the strength of changing his/her world or the world he/she lives in with the passion of bright stars to keep on going and thriving for excellence..

in my own structuring motivational dreamer staircase to a heaven of joy and the beautiful art of shaping ALAMINOS, ---I will join you in your dream where there is no space of imagination ever from hereon----"No Importation of Basura"

You did mention that it is mandated by DENR that every municipality and city to have sanitary landfill... GOOD NEWS---that means, every city and municipality has that big responsibility of taking care of their own "basura" and that is very defining and even more concrete---Alaminos should never ever allow importation of "basura" ---no more excuse(s) why we be responsible for other region's toxicities and waste eliminations ---not in Alaminos, not in our book to follow----for Alaminos should preserve it's perfect beauty and the easence of a green haven of many hopes and aspirations. Live and enjoy and seek better options.

Dream big and it is free but your dream is so precious to us as well as to "yourself," and being the leader of our town, keep that strength of your Dream as a dreamer and as a Model of Productivity and in keeping Alaminos beautiful----keep your music alive as you continue to dream big and join us in our most historical dream ever ---"No Importation of Basura"---and let it be the rhythm of a storyline in an embarking episode of your most concluding dream of a legacy to share upon your people and we.will. all be glad we made it through struggling activities.

Maraming Salamat po....GOD bless.

A landfill will never be a compromise in Alaminos, Laguna. The hazardous impact on our health and environment will be a trademark of an ill-reputed and stinky **governance that allowed accumulation of garbage in our finest greens and pristine** rivers and bodies of water, exploiting our mother earth. And, it will not take its course in our voice of freedom instilled with wisdom and conviction for the love of our ancestral home to ever become a reality. A resounding voice bound in unity and trust for one another—is an outloud blast and an uproar to a shout of a "No to Landfill." Together under one mission of a stronghold and faith—we will triumph till the end. Never to lose hope—there is a paradise in our world of love and commitment to our ancestry and many generations from here and onwards...... God bless Alaminos.

"Importation of other waste materials or *garbage* from neighboring towns is not a compromise. We should take care of our own *garbage*. Two truckloads per day is the amount of our *garbage*. Discipline is another major key to exercise to avoid unnecessary accumulation of *garbage*."

Nida Bejosano Goudeaux

AModérateur • À l'instant

As we empower our living advocacy, we also have to adhere to leadership that will promote peace, unity, and prosperity toward achieving our goals. We followers must reconcile our thoughts with spiritual engagement and accountability to our own cause of expression and self-willing actions. Let us unify and be willing to compromise with the opposition that we will all be encouraged to work together and strive for economic growth and not embrace one-sided self-interests that will only benefit a few, especially only those in power. but will be dismantled by the majority as they are hovered by darkness where their moral conscience is at their most prosecuting state of guilt. There is no turning back for the legacy that is to be dreamt of will be lost in reality and is never to be remembered for there is nothing for another chance to look back---so my suggestion, be with us in our most advocating choice of being a true-blooded Alaminos fellow---we ought to be one, for the grace of the beauty inherent upon us....

Alaminos, GOD first.

Nida Bejosano Goudeaux

Modérateur • 18 h

THE REAL MEANING OF HISTORY OF ALAMINOS REMARKABLY BEGINS IN ALL OF "No to Landfill" ADVOCATES ---

The true heroes, the real fighters of truth and good cause---"for the love and prosperity of Alaminos"----resides in you, in all of you, in all of us who have given ourselves the challenge to create our Hall of Liberty, our Chamber of Democracy, our Spiritual Upliftment and our Unity to hail out loud our freedom of being heard and being proud of ourselves as ONE.

Let us not forget that despite political and personal issues and differences, which are just normal things in life, and Alaminos is not an exceptional case, there are still those people in the government, in the local structure of our town, who had proven to us their most genuine intent and that they also struggle in unity with us to support our advocacy. I won't mention names for we all know who they are. Let us applaud them, though it is their public duty, but the point is they still stood firm to their convictions of being just and true. They were attributes in our remarkable fight so to speak. And let us stay positive that those with clear conscience stay faithful forever in their public service.

Let us not forget the continuing tasks involved, which are being fulfilled by those volunteers, especially out there in Alaminos, who are physically, tirelessly, and unconditionally laboring and dedicating their service to give their very best to obtain our biggest goal and succeed. Even in extremely tropical climate, where the sun beams to their faces, they are exposing themselves to get through the day and continue on without any emotional outbursts of qualms, complains, or negativity. They are dead serious to succeed.

Let us offer ourselves continuously and to pray without ceasing that a miracle happens. Let us pray that the one leading Die Hard hinker(s) still embracing "No to Objection" will sometime realize the spiritual importance of his/their moral responsibility of being an advocate for what is right, what is just, and what the people of Alaminos are truly looking forward to—an advocacy that is best and excellent for Alaminos.

Further, I need not repeat what this whole program of life well-projected vision we have installed upon us---for We, the people of our finest green town are on the same page embracing the truth and the proudest to proclaim a remarkable history of our all generations of Alaminos we created in our most spiritual and visible engagement of our heroic acts, True gifts of Alaminos.

Alaminos, GOD first!

Thank you to all of you who have enjoyed reading my long and lengthy postings. *Pasensya na po.*

Egay De Villa It is very ironic to see the very people mandated to protect our town and those we entrusted the future of our children were unmasked as the true oppressors clad in public servant's clothing.

Thanks to ordinary citizens from all walks of life, who trooped to the streets in response to call for genuine heroism to protect our beloved Alaminos.

The evil intention of those in power is not sleeping, but let us all warn them in resounding voice not to underestimate the power of masses.

Nida Beiosano Goudeaux þ Egay De Villa There will be light after dawn and there will be no denial of spiritual engagement when the verdict of truth revealed their true colors. Let us stay Positive in our Advocacy and may their be no statutory of limitations to capture their moral conscience as they move forward for a better mind-set of their own.

"DISIPLINA ANG TUNAY NA SUSI TUNGO SA KAUNLARAN"

Nida Bejosano Goudeaux

Modérateur • 4 janvier, 13:05

"BE VIGILANT, ASSERTIVE, CONCRETE, OBJECTIVE, AND CONSTRUCTIVE."

"NO TO LANDFILL" ENCOURAGES GOOD LIFE AND GOOD LIVING. UNITY IS THE KEY.

BE VIGILANT, ASSERTIVE, CONCRETE, OBJECTIVE, AND CONSTRUCTIVE. "NO TO LANDFILL" ENCOURAGES GOOD LIFE AND GOOD LIVING. UNITY IS THE KEY.

Nida Bejosano Goudeaux

Modérateur • 2 h

CHECKER'S CHAMPION—LET IT BE IN THE SPIRIT OF DILIGENCE TO WIN OVER OUR GREATEST ADVOCACY. BE VIGILANT. Alaminos, GOD first!

Nida Bejosano Goudeaux

6 November 2019 •

Change.org

Landfill will never be a compromise in Alaminos, Laguna. The disastrous impact on our health and environment will be a trademark of an ill-reputed and stinky governance in allowing accumulation of garbage in our finest greens and pristine wealth on rivers and bodies of water to monopolize our mother earth and, it will not take its course in our voice of freedom instilled with wisdom and conviction for the love of our ancestral home to ever become a reality. A resounding voice bound in unity and trust for one another—is an outloud blast and an uproar to a shout of a "No to Landfill." Together under one mission of a stronghold and faith—we will triumph till the end. Never to lose hope—there is a paradise in our world of love and commitment to our ancestry and many generations from here and onwards...... God bless Alaminos.

A ONE LIFE TO LIVE

SPARE THE LIVELIHOOD OF ALAMINOS THE JOB OPPORTUNITY FROM LANDFILL HEALTH IS AT RISK.

"No to Landfill."

Nida Bejosano Goudeaux

Modérateur • 32 min

"A bitter refrain is not a remedy to a fight for a great rallying advocacy. Focus on positivity...a unifying spirit and a word of wisdom uplifts the integrity of a visionary mission..."

Wake up with a cheerful pose and approach a daily living with a morning delight that savors the sweet taste of life.....GOD bless.

Susan Fandiño Vivid, lucid & positive...well said!

Egay De Villa þ Nice. The message is very healing. Let's move on very productively.

Nida Bejosano Goudeaux þ kaya nga....parang capitalization or impact is focused on the history and story line of bashings---it seems vengeance is just boiling from within...can it not be a sorrow of the past and be buried? Move on and carry the torch of advocacy without any qualms of bitterness, speculations but instead an honest approach to fight a good and just cause to life-living in Alaminos? But, make sure there is that logic and wisdom of truth----and no ulterior motives whatsoever...election and campaign has it's own timeline....."No to Landfill" is the greatest honor of our image and a defining legacy one holds with the clean and pure intent of a dream fulfilling and all....Egay we are always on the same page ha???

Nida Bejosano Goudeaux

Modérateur • 6 h

Though it is understandable that RA 9003 is endeavored of providing for an Ecological Solid Waste Management, still it is a "no brainer," Alaminos is not a suitable place for any high level scale of sanitary landfill. Level 4 is completely out of the picture, an absolute no, right? And I think it had been long established. Why still get puzzled?

Solid Waste Management based on the research I did work on and everyone is aware of this---the main goal of which is to protect and safeguard public health and restore a superior quality of life and live to the expectation of being eco-friendly. However, let me reiterate, Alaminos is not the place to establish landfill on a high scale. This is a given scenario based on the supposedly planned landfill sites as proposed perhaps by investors who were/are eyeing for Alaminos to be the targeted spot on sanitary landfill development. No way will this be approved by the clamoring citizenry of Alaminos. Let us stay proactive as advocates of "No to Landfill." Stay vigilant but not reactionary to trigger retaliations of brain wars among the two opposing factions ("No to Landfill" and "No to Objection"). Let us compromise, for they are also residents (Pro-Landfill) who will be affected by the toxic or adverse effects of garbage or waste materials as well and will suffer the same consequences, and they better believe it. Equal inhalation of toxins or chemical substances disastrous to health will impact the entire population of our township, and this is the reason why we should all oppose the sanitary landfill on a high level. This is an alert system that should alarm those still in the dark and thinking otherwise for sanitary landfill on high scale. It is not a wise option to undertake.

Discipline is the key element in this fair game. Let no land or body of water be dumped with any form of garbage/waste materials. It pollutes the environment even more. There's got to be a strict implementation of this rule in order to carry out an efficient method of waste management, one way or the other. This will begin from its inception to its final disposal, and the methods should clearly be observed in order for us to effectively be in our adhering act of not polluting or causing more toxins floating in the air or any underground contaminations. We want to preserve our nature's best so we be the first to advocate cleanliness of our surrounding and strict implementation within our own backyard and front yard. The foundation of our advocacy should start in our own occupied shelter. Do you guys agree with me? I do follow this house rule in my daily tasks. This is where I am very strict and meticulous.

I think the LGU was required by law to formulate a ten-year solid waste management plan (my understanding), and it is supposed to be reviewed every two years, and it is mandated and still in effect, but our LGU has not done any review yet. (This is in my understanding. Please feel free to correct me on this matter in case I am contradicting or not accurate on this specific situation.) This is a vehicle to adhere so as to comply with greener and protective safeguard on our environment.

Bottomline, improper disposal of municipal waste is unsanitary and can cause outbreaks in the form of many health risks or illnesses and can pose danger in our economy, social living, and many more adverse effects. *Kaya sama-sama po tayong itaguyod and tamang disiplina habang ang ating advokasiya ay ating tuluyan rin pong isinusulong.*

Our own "basura" is our main target. *Yan po ang ating objective*, and let us be vigilant and assertive without causing troubles or further confusion. *Yon lang po at Maraming Salamat.*

Nida Bejosano Goudeaux

Modérateur • 14 h

What will define Alaminos to our future generations? There are many hard choices to make, and we have to face our truths.

Let us take part with courage and wisdom, and let us allow our empowering citizens, leaders, activists, reformists, organizers, and problem solvers to undertake the challenges and fate of our locality. Let us build our future and begin to accept and engage into a shared responsibility and to a greater degree of moderation achieve prosperity without damaging one's integrity or reputation especially those who exhibited the accomplished mission of our truest advocacy and let us not forget that as well. At the same time, let our journey for a clean campaign to invite investors that will protect the beauty of our heritage and our culture be the biggest factor of adhering first and foremost As we continue to proceed with a pursuit to succeed our greatest hope of just having our own "Basura"—— let us think of added revenue-driven machine or resolutions that can push our hope to reality or prosperity to appease the noise(s)/commotions and calm down our citizenry and at the same time let those in public service come into their enlightening position as we integrate our plan of actions towards one common and ideal goal to eliminate completely fractions concerning landfill issues. There has to be an ideal and conforming guidance of a common and universal principle——which is to abide by what could serve best for our town and it's people. I stay consistent with my most unifying and undying prayerful task as I fly upon my own wing of hopes with all of you out there carrying the same advocacy which is A Better Life Today and the Futures.

Nida Bejosano Goudeaux

Modérateur • 14 h

What will define Alaminos to our future generations? There are many hard choices to make and we have to face our truths.

Let us take part with courage & wisdom and let us allow our empowering citizens, leaders, activists, reformists, organizers and problem solvers to undertake the challenges and fate of our locality. Let us build our future and begin to accept and engage into a shared responsibility and to a greater degree of moderation achieve prosperity without damaging one's integrity or reputation especially those who exhibited the accomplished mission of our truest advocacy and let us not forget that as well. At the same time, let our journey for a clean campaign to invite investors that will protect and restore our heritage of our culture be the biggest factor of adhering to it first and foremost. Let us continue to proceed with a pursuit to succeed our greatest hope of just having our own "Basura"--- let us think of added revenue-driven machine or resolutions that can push our hope to reality or prosperity to appease the noise(s)/ commotions and calm down our citizenry and at the same time let those in public service come into their enlightening position as we integrate our plan of actions towards one common and ideal goal to eliminate completely fractions concerning landfill issues. There has to be an ideal and conforming guidance of a common and universal principle--which is for the welfare of our people, plain and simple. I stay consistent with my most unifying and undying prayerful task as I fly upon my own wing of hopes with all of you out there carrying the same advocacy which is A Better Life Today and the Futures.

The environmental challenges is not a responsibility tasked upon to our community
It is a liability to be undertaken with courteous decline of the majority
And undoubtedly considered a major health hazard and we were not brought up
To a town where we breathe not only congestion but infestation being such a worst scenario
We dare not allow such a project to be in our territory for it is a "trash" accumulation
Unwanted and rejected by all means – and "WE SHOULD UNITE" all together
To a One Voice – **"A clean and fresh environment"** where we all deserve a loud whisper
One town, One Community, One cheerful statement with a firm stand—**"No to Landfill"**
It is not acceptable in any form of living right here in our "town of Alaminos"
And together, let our voices be heard and let a triumphant victory be the voice for all
"No to Landfill"

The emotional wholeness is best achieved by not allowing the weight of guilt and condemnation to be the wreckage of a refreshing start. The bitterness and negativity of your distressful encounters be a learning conservation of your productivity in the next chapter of your adventure either you are in your own comfort zone or in your own exploratory zone. Be unceasing to discover what is the next goal or worth of space for the engine that will keep your motivation up and about all depends on what you have truly experienced and that will give you many insights of "push overs" mechanisms---such a derivative of life with many ingredients to spice the wheel of fortune as it moves in different directions----a choice you will make....just make sure prudence becomes your light of guidance.

Personally, I do not engage much with not cleansing my spirit for I find it useless and not sincere at all---I do try to live with the grace of humility and the grace of generosity—to hold me tight while I search for more truth in me. I am not conceived without original sin for I have my own share of guilt, imperfections and sinful thoughts but I do try to not make excuses for myself—saying, it is just but human we make mistakes because having that kind of reasoning is not an admiring level up thoughts—it is adding more injury to one's wrongdoings. The best approach is not to entertain excuses that will invite more invasion of unrighteousness.

If we confess our sins, He is faithful and just to forgive us our sins

And to cleanse us from all unrighteousness

1 John 1:9 ESV

A woman in the window---with a *M*illion and the sweetest smile at broad day light
So *I*nviting, so demure, so consistent, soft-spoken, so polite, so tactful, and so pure at heart
How could I not thank her for she is so *M*erciful, humble, dignified, giving, and compassionate?
With the *I*deology of a strong and faithful involvement "No to Landfill" as her advocate task
There is that winning battle of mind that cooperates with her silent but overwhelming spirit
Of faith and hope though her emotions remain balanced and secured for she
Believes there is that perfect timing when all the oppositions
And the advocates will at some point recognized
The one intent of a pleasant finest green
To be the epitome lasting and all

As it combines with her assets
Of perfect thoughts and hopes

Her participation to "No to Landfill"—accelerates the strength in a woman's good temper of behavior with comments on social media so gracefully expressed. There is that impact of sincerity and an increased level of sensitivity of the subject matter that becomes a crucial affected and sad refrain of her spiraling downward of normal doubts. But she exhibits her worries with prayers on her side to support the majority of town folks with her prayerful yet physical engagement in meetings held here in our destination from across thousand of miles from our protests emerging out there in Alaminos, Laguna. Her gentle ways and untiring self is challenged by the reality of a thunderstorm-like shock that has triggered us from here abroad and still left us with worrying responses of a battle that is not equipped yet of clear directions for there are no set leaders to start the protest against the "pro-landfill" enthusiasts. She and I are in constant communication and are affected and hoping against hope that all those virtues of love put to love---for our preservation of the beauty of our town and bind us all together perhaps in perfect unity to steal our joy once succumbed into this inevitable project of Berjaya that has been so disturbing, controversial, and critical in the living situations especially those who are living in our town. It will be a long-suffering of disastrous representation of Berjaya and could be the end powering of our immense beauty of our fine green environment. This calamity of nature extracted by Berjaya with the strong-will inclusion of those souls living in the dark and the group of "No to Objection" on landfill ---will take its course in a hell-bent selfish interest which is rejected or opposed with upheavals and bustling noises from social media, on the ground force in the town proper and mobilized by the power of protest from within the outside world. She prays fervently that Sanitary Landfill be confined solely for our own trash prevention and custody.

*W*inning the uproar of her battling yet advocating assertion
Comes through an *A*dorable woman equipped with virtues installed
*Y*earning to reach out through the grief and sorrow of many agonizing living souls
With bustling words of her own decisive disposition to reject the *N*uisance of dirty tricks
*I*solationist is not in her personal profile of a conduct or defined behavior
Well behaved set of life standards is her rule towards progressing---an *E*nlightening throne
A gracious voice on a woman's body nourished upon her own instilled
Power of intelligence, wisdom, and vastness of experiences
And could not be trampled by incriminating actions but empowered by kind gestures
Life proceeds in many great moves
Such is that strong will power that prolongs in her latitude of many successes
A woman of a dignifying soul with pride and dignity upon her shoulder of many responsibilities
and Christian baptized with devotion of a sanctity of true inspiration and powerful thoughts

---

In the midst of a suffering town, there is that thankful chapter that came out of the blue and reaching out due to insurmountable pressures that have agonized the many hidden flaws where wickedness of the wicked in the chamber (legislative in nature) I addressed to in the hall of the town municipality prevailed in bustling and combative attacks from the general public---but there I found a friend in her, grasping the roots of embracing ancestry of no biological interest but of common fraction "No to Landfill"---A beautiful lad in her duty of womanhood and responsible citizenry creates a big vacuum of my inner core of dignity and profound liberty of mind and heart of same expectations and degree of involvement with intensity of blessed thoughts and words acclaimed. We joined together as best of friends and best friends forever in an unfailing abounds of our initiatives, determination and commitment to be advocates in our own strength and in a circumstance that faced the nation of our life in motion. "No to Landfill"--- becomes our modus operandi of our geared friendship initiating and belonging to one another as town folks in our Paradise of Treasures---Alaminos, Laguna our birthplace, our very own.

She and I are in constant communication and are affected and hoping against hope that all those virtues of love put to love---for our preservation of the beauty of our town and bind us all together perhaps in perfect unity to steal our joy once succumbed into this inevitable project of Berjaya that has been so disturbing, controversial, and critical in the living situations especially those who are living in our town. It will be a long-suffering of disastrous representation of Berjaya and could be the end powering of our immense beauty of our fine green environment. This calamity of nature extracted by Berjaya with the strong-will inclusion of those souls living in the dark and the group of "No to Objection" on landfill ---will take its course in a hell-bent selfish interest which is rejected or opposed with upheavals and bustling noises from social media, on the ground force in the town proper and mobilized by the power of protest from within the outside world. She prays fervently that Sanitary Landfill be confined solely for our own trash prevention and custody.

A guy with an "*E*ndearing" expression of kindness and admiration
Such is "*G*entleman" in a living color that captures oneness as a bonding progress
In an "*A*dvocating" participation "No to Landfill" and bridge upon a common factor
Of a mission where-"*You*" and I collaborate to reach the mountain peak of our noble task
To express upon our loudest participation in a recognition of our true faith to make
ALAMINOS the most treasured and finest ancestral home of our generations and the next
To be in a stillness while in a thriving economic growth
And together we can hail upon triumph
As we thank the LORD for the gift

With ancestry of some generations left behind
There still goes the affectionate retrospect regardless for we honor the history
As we look upon yesterday to bring upon today the endless cherishing story notes of then
There was this start up conversations that never ceased even until now
Of the living past of our ancestors while in heaven they are made to rest
While we don't bother to call it quits even because we think of always think of them
For they represent the milestones of thousands loves and fairy tales of their past
But now we join hands and create a history and a story of our own
While we cradle the foundation and the institution of their integrity and worth
And in you my new-found friend---there is a revelation of our true colors
We are ONE in ONE Spirit of hope and advocacy
"No to Landfill"---still, reminds us
To combine our thoughts and force into this whole ballgame with love and unity at most

ENJOY A SHORT ADVENTURE

OF MY "INTERIOR DESIGN"

A PASSION NURTURED THROUGH TIME

A PASSION EXHIBITED THROUGH SELF-GRATIFICATION

A PASSION EMBRACED INTO A SELF-DEFINING STYLE

TRULY INSPIRING

Nida Bejosano Goudeaux

26 October 2019

A virtual tour...in a re-decorating mode...just a believer. I could produce a colorful tone and do some sort of mix and match and have a sense of self-gratification special way to be a push over in an effort to present a touch of my passion. I discovered I could put together some passionate and gracious creation in an artistic .style without any idea from before that I could be a possible artist in my own stylish way. I owe this manifested skills from being exposed to many homes as a realtor and as an enthusiast, for I was once limited in having enough resources to allocate a masterpiece in interior design mode outside my own privileged opportunities from this modest living. Perseverance and a good attitude reflected despite many hurdles exposed drove me to a paradise of new discovery and a challenging freedom of life-changing. Pardon me as I enjoy creative writing and designs.

Nida Bejosano Goudeaux

Modérateur • 7 février, 16:19

Good afternoon, fellow classmates and all my "kababayan." Though I am not physically present there with you or not physically within your reach, nevertheless, I am in the nearness of a spiritual engagement to present to your heart this very exciting and memorable fiftieth class reunion of batch 1964-1970. To me, we are so blessed to have been graciously given this opportunity to have an amazing celebration. We survived good times and bad, and life moved us forward to our own paths and destinations. We made it through.

Elementary days are nostalgic. They are full of lively and a happy memories, making me wish I am still there, but life travels in many directions. It has been several decades since we all started to attend school at Alaminos Elementary School. We were so young then and just happy, but we now love and enjoy the fond memories of it. Certainly, though, we got into this stage of our lives where everyone has a family of their own and a life to live. We are lucky enough as we have stretched out our life span this far. Let us keep going, keep on living with love and peace in pursuit of more success.

My memories of Alaminos are always the wonderful living colors of my childhood. I was playful girl who could beat many boys of my age or even older in outdoor games. The plaza was my joyful domain. Being a poor girl that I was in a very simple way of living I was fortunate as I was tendered with love and joy from my family. Our neighbors were simple too and we just enjoyed our community with a peaceful taking every bit of the way. I will never forget the growing stages of my life, playful and exciting and when I moved to Manila, there I found the busy dynamic of day-to-day living but I remained the simple girl that I was.....no partying still but pretty much purely engaged in school and pursuing higher education which became the instrumental privilege that anchored me through another destination America, that is... Here in the States, I get to know the challenges and the many potentials of greener pastures. Sacrificial living encouraged me to keep going and striving and thriving gets me to my most promising endeavors----real estate, home care business and being a professional writer here in the U.S. keeps me more inspired and more fulfilling....And this is where the strength of my being, my mission in life has geared me to a more benevolent response inherent since I was little. Poverty challenged me to keep me going but with virtues instilled upon me as my guiding light—my parents had pridefully endowed to us. I have some flaws and share of imperfections of my own just like everyone else, but I thrived to be the best I could be. And live up to the expectations of being the hardworking person that I could always be. I survived the tests of times, thank GOD. My anchor of strength and hope and fulfillment---all coming from our Dear LORD especially when I was in my cancer journey and my quest, then and now...and the next chapter is to continue advocating for love and sharing.

Now, my visionary self becomes a vehicle for my strongest advocacy---which is "No to Landfill" of which I have the loudest and most affirmative convictions of my own disciplinary and

COOKING IS MY PASSION

PHOTO SECTION

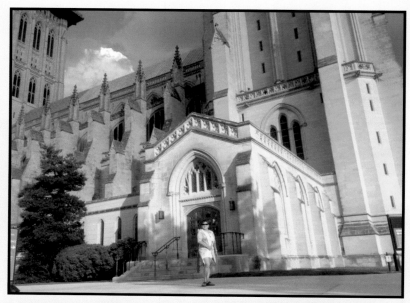

Printed in the United States
By Bookmasters